ISBN 978-0-266-81090-2
PIBN 10893011

ATH'ᴸ RUSSELL STURGIS

WITH A BRIEF INTRODUCTORY SKETCH OF HIS ANCESTORS
IN ENGLAND AND THE MASSACHUSETTS COLONY

BOSTON
NINETEEN HUNDRED

INTRODUCTION.

ξ STURGIS OF CLIPSTON had a son RICHARD STURGIS OF CLIPSTON, from whor
ΞIS OF CLIPSTON, who was the father of ROBERT STURGIS OF FAXTON, whose so:
ΛNNINGTON, whose son EDWARD STURGIS emigrated to New England about 1635, ;
n EDWARD STURGIS, JR., went to New England with his father, and settled in Yar
American branch and father of THOMAS STURGIS (*1st generation*), who died 1708, and ν
:neration), born 1686.

MAS STURGIS (*2d generation*), born at Yarmouth, April 14, 1686. Died at Barnstabl
Iarried Dec. 26, 1717, Martha Russell
Barnstable. She died June 17, 1774,
ι her 78th year.
children were (*3d generation*):

rtha	born Nov. 19, 1718	died N
abeth	June 12, 1721	Æ
omas, Jr.	July 22, 1722	C
abeth	Aug. 26, 1725	Ϊ
iarried Apr. 19, 1752, Thomas Allen		
Barnstable, and had three children		
ho died young.		
ecca	Oct. 9, 1727	J
ithan	June 17, 1730	J
gail	July 22, 1732	J
inah	Aug. 24, 1735	J

	born	died
RUSSELL STURGIS (*4th generation*), third child of Thomas, Jr., and Sarah, married Nov. 13, 1773, Elizabeth Perkins of Boston.	Aug. 27, 1750	Sept. 7, 1i
	Jan. 18, 1756	Sept. 18, 1i
Their children were (*5th generation*):		
1 James Perkins	Oct. 21, 1774	———, 1:
2 Elizabeth Peck	Apr. 22, 1776	Aug. 11, 1
3 Elizabeth Peck	June 13, 1777	Oct. 11, 1:
4 Nathaniel Russell	Feb. 17, 1779	Sept. 27, 1i
5 Thomas	Aug. 16, 1781	Aug. 11, 1
6 Elizabeth Perkins	Apr. 9, 1783	Aug. 27, 1
7 Charles	Aug. 19, 1784	Sept. 20, 1i
8 Sarah Paine	Apr. 18, 1786	June 12, 1i
9 Elizabeth Perkins	Apr. 27, 1787	Feb. 10, 1:
10 Eliza	Dec. 30, 1788	Mar. 20, 1i
11 Henry	Feb. 13, 1790	Apr. 11, 1i
12 James Perkins	July 9, 1791	Aug. 24, 1i
13 George Washington	Oct. 5, 1793	Sept. 5, 1i
14 Ann Perkins	Jan. 31, 1795	Feb. 6, 1:
15 Ann Cushing	Apr. 30, 1797	Jan. 4, 1i
16 Mary Perkins	May 14, 1800	Sept. 2, 1i

FOURTH GENERATION NOTES.

From **William**, the second child of Thomas, Jr., are descended Mrs. Robert G Shaw, Mrs. Robert and Mrs. Samuel Hooper, William Sturgis Bigelow, Mrs. Tappan and her issue, also Isaac Hinckley and his issue.

From **Thomas**, the fifth child, are descended Russell and William Sturgis of New York, and numerous descendants, Barney &

From **Samuel**, the eighth child, are descended many children. The eldest, Lucretia, was Mrs. Joshua Bates of London, f Madame Sylvain Van der Weyer (Elizabeth Ann Sturgis Bates), and issue, now living in England Captain Josiah Sturgis, Un Cutter, was son of this **Samuel**.

FIFTH GENERATION NOTES.

James Perkins, the first child of Russell and Elizabeth, sailed for St. Domingo in November or December, 1790, and was n nor the ship in which he sailed. Two children only of Russell left issue, **Nathaniel Russell**, fourth child, who married Susan **Cushing**, fifteenth child, who married Frederic William Paine. **Sarah**, the eighth, and **George W.**, the thirteenth child, had issue

THE DESCENDANTS OF
NATH'ᴸ RUSSELL STURGIS

EDITION OF ONE HUNDRED COPIES, PRINTED
AT BOSTON BY GEORGE H ELLIS

NATH'ᴸ RUSSELL STURGIS:
HJS SONS AND DAUGHTERS.

NATHANIEL RUSSELL STURGIS
b. Feb. 17, 1779.
m. Sept. 11, 1804, *Susan Parkman*
d. Sept. 27, 1856.   *d. Oct. 16, 1827.*

RUSSELL (A 1) *
b. July 7, 1805.
m. Apr. 3, 1828, *Lucy Lyman Paine*
                d. Aug. 23, 1828.
m. Sept. 28, 1829, *Mary Greene Hubbard*
                d. Sept. 17, 1837.
m. June 4, 1846, *Julia O. Boit*
d. Nov. 2, 1887.   *d. May 1, 1888.*

HENRY PARKMAN (A 2)
b. Oct. 13, 1806.
m. Mar. 5, 1835, *Mary Georgiana Howard.*
                d. Feb. 25, 1850.
m. Aug. 14, 1851, *Elizabeth Orne Paine.*
d. Dec. 15, 1869.

SAMUEL PARKMAN (A 3)
b. Feb. 18, 1808.
d. Feb. 18, 1877.

ELIZABETH PERKINS (A 4)
b. Aug. 30, 1809.
m. Dec. 3, 1832, *Henry Grew*
d. Jan. 27, 1848.   *d. Jan. 16, 1892.*

SUSAN PARKMAN (A 5)
b. Dec. 3, 1810.
m. Nov. 26, 1835, *John Parkman*
d. Jan. 11, 1869.   *d. Sept. 24, 1883.*

SARAH BLAKE (A 6)
b. Dec. 4, 1812.
d. Oct. 11, 1814.

CHARLES JAMES (A 7)
b. Mar. 13, 1814.
d. Dec. 30, 1823.

SARAH BLAKE (A 8)
b. Aug. 31, 1815.
m. June 9, 1835, *Francis George Shaw*
                d. Nov. 7, 1882.

GEORGE (A 9)
b. Apr. 22, 1817.
m. Apr. 22, 1849, *Josefina Borras.*
d. July 7, 1857.

HARRIETT TILDEN (A 10)
b. Nov. 8, 1820.
m. May 7, 1846, *William Abijah White*
d. Mar. 12, 1850.   *d. Oct. 10, 1856.*

JAMES (A 11)
b. Aug. 22, 1822.
m. Oct. 8, 1845, *Mary Catharine Townsend*
d. Jan. 21, 1888.   *d. Nov. 15, 1887.*

ROBERT SHAW (A 12)
b. Aug. 29, 1824.
m. Oct. 4, 1858, *Susan Brimmer Inches.*
d. Apr. 2, 1876.

I

NATH'L RUSSELL STURGIS:
HIS CHILDREN AND GRANDCHILDREN.

RUSSELL STURGIS (A 1)
b. July 7, 1805.
m. Apr. 3, 1828, *Lucy Lyman Paine*
     d. *Aug.* 23, 1828.

m. Sept. 28, 1829, *Mary Greene Hubbard*
     d. *Sept.* 17, 1837.

m. June 4, 1846, *Julia O. Boit*
d. Nov. 2, 1887.   d. *May 1, 1888.*

RUSSELL, JR. (A 1, B 1)
b. Aug. 3, 1831.
m. July 14, 1856, *Susan Welles*
     d. *Dec. 12, 1862.*
m. May 29, 1866, *Margery McCulloh.*
d. Oct. 14, 1899.

LUCY LYMAN PAINE (A 1, B 2)
b. Mar. 13, 1833.
m. Feb. 28, 1856, *Charles Russell Codman.*

JOHN HUBBARD (A 1, B 3)
b. Aug. 5, 1834.
m. Sept. 14, 1858, *Frances Anne Codman.*
d. Feb. 14, 1888.

MARY GREENE (A 1, B 4)
b. June 18, 1837.
d. Apr. 28, 1838.

HENRY PARKMAN, II. (A 1, B 5)
b. Mar. 1, 1847.
m. Oct. 2, 1872, *Mary Cecilia Brand*
     d. *June 18, 1886.*
m. July 17, 1894, *Marie Eveleen Meredith.*

JULIAN RUSSELL (A 1, B 6)
b. Oct. 21, 1848.
m. Nov. 8, 1883, *Mary Maud Beresford.*

MARY GREENE HUBBARD (A 1, B 7)
b. Feb 2, 1851.
m. July 5, 1871, *Leopold Richard Seymour.*

HOWARD OVERING (A 1, B 8)
b. Nov. 8, 1855.

GEORGE ROBERT RUSSELL (A 2, B 1)
b. May 25, 1836.
d. Dec. 11, 1865.

MARY HOWARD (A 2, B 2)
b. Dec. 8, 1837.
d. Dec. 12, 1837.

HENRY HOWARD (A 2, B 3)
b. Nov. 5, 1838.
m. Nov. 5, 1863, *Caroline Augusta Manson*
d. Jan. 31, 1881.   *d. Oct. 31, 1880.*

JAMES PERKINS (A 2, B 4)
b. Oct 29, 1839.
d. Sept. 8, 1840.

JAMES PERKINS (A 2, B 5)
b. Oct. 14, 1841.
d. Jan. 2, 1864.

CHARLES EDWARD (A 2, B 6)
b. July 31, 1843.
d. Aug. 4, 1843.

FREDERICK RUSSELL (A 2, B 7)
b. July 7, 1844.
m. Apr. 6, 1870, *Martha De Wolf Hazard.*

MARY TRINIDAD HOWARD (A 2, B 8)
b. July 26, 1848.
m. Apr. 18, 1881, *Samuel George Chetwynd Middlemore*
d. Feb. 11, 1890.   *d. Jan. 27, 1890.*

3)

NATH'L RUSSELL STURGIS:
HIS CHILDREN AND GRANDCHILDREN.

ELIZABETH PERKINS STURGIS (A 4)
b. Aug. 30, 1809.
m. Dec. 3, 1832, *Henry Grew*
d. Jan. 27, 1848.   *d. Jan. 16, 1892.*

HENRY STURGIS (A 4, B 1)
b. Jan. 23, 1834.
m. Dec. 20, 1863, *Jane Norton Wigglesworth.*

CHARLES JAMES (A 4, B 2)
b. Jan. 14, 1836.
d. Mar. 17, 1850.

EDWARD STURGIS (A 4, B 3)
b. Mar. 10, 1842.
m. Nov. 26, 1867, *Annie Crawford Clark.*

ELIZABETH PERKINS (A 4, B 4)
b. July 14, 1845.
d. Jan. 16, 1889.

SUSAN PARKMAN STURGIS (A 5)
b. Dec. 3, 1810.
m. Nov. 26, 1835, *John Parkman*
d. Jan. 11, 1869.   *d. Sept. 24, 1883.*

THEODORE (A 5, B 1)
b. Jan. 22, 1837.
killed in battle, Dec. 16, 1862.

MARY RUSSELL (A 5, B 2)
b. Aug. 8, 1838.

SUSAN (A 5, B 3)
b. Nov. 6, 1839.
d. June 3, 1850.

ALICE (A 5, B 4)
b. May 6, 1844.
m. Jan. 7, 1878, *William Smith Carter.*

BERTHA STURGIS (A 5, B 5)
b. Sept. 30, 1849.
d. Oct. 14, 1875.

RUSSELL STURGIS:
EN AND GRANDCHILDREN.

ANNA (A 8, B 1)
b. Apr. 9, 1836.
m. Nov. 28, 1856, *George William Curtis*
          d. Aug. 31, 1892.

ROBERT GOULD (A 8, B 2)
b. Oct. 10, 1837.
m. May 2, 1863, *Annie Haggerty.*
killed in battle July 18, 1863.

SUSANNA (A 8, B 3)
b. May 31, 1839.
m. Oct. 31, 1862, *Robert B. Minturn*
          d. Dec. 15, 1889.

JOSEPHINE (A 8, B 4)
b. Dec. 16, 1843.
m. Oct. 30, 1863, *Charles Russell Lowell, Jr.*
          killed in battle, Oct. 20, 1864.

ELLEN (A 8, B 5)
b. July 1, 1845.
m. Oct. 24, 1867, *Francis Channing Barlow*
          d. Jan. 11, 1896.

NATH'ᴸ RUSSELL STUR
HIS CHILDREN AND GRANDCHIL

GEORGE STURGIS (A 9)
b. Apr. 22, 1817.
m. Apr. 22, 1849, *Josefina Borras*.
d. July 7, 1857.

JOSEPH BORRAS (A 9, B 1)
b. Mar. 8, 1850.
d. Oct. 8, 1852.

SUSAN PARKMAN (A 9, B 2)
b. June 6, 1851.
m. Nov. 26, 1892, *Celedonio Sastre*.

JOSEFINA BORRAS (A 9, B 3)
b. June 29, 1853.

ROBERT SHAW, II. (A 9, B 4)
b. Nov. 21, 1854.
m. Apr. 9, 1890, *Ellen Gardner Hodges*.

JAMES VICTOR (A 9, B 5)
b. Oct. 18, 1856.
d. May 27, 1858.

HARRIETT TILDEN STURGIS (A 10)
b. Nov. 8, 1820.
m. May 7, 1846, *William Abijah White*
d. Mar. 12, 1850.   *d. Oct. 10, 1856.*

WILLIAM HOWARD (A 10, B 1)
b. Feb. 21, 1847.
m. Oct. 8, 1878, *Margaret Parker*.
d. Dec 11, 1895.

AMY (A 10, B 2)
b. Sept. 25, 1848.

JAMES STURGIS (A 11)
b. Aug. 22, 1822.
m. Oct. 8, 1845, *Mary Catharine Townsend.*
d. Jan. 21, 1888.   *d. Nov. 15, 1887.*

SUSAN (A 11, B 1)
b. Sept. 7, 1846.
m. Jan. 16, 1867, *Henry Horton McBurne*
        d. Feb. 10, 1875.
m. May 3, 1876, *Henry Bigelow Williams*

CHARLES WILKINS (A 11, B 2)
b. May 29, 1849.

FRANCIS SHAW (A 11, B 3)
b. Aug. 15, 1853.

ROBERT SHAW STURGIS (A 12)
b. Aug. 29, 1824.
m. Oct. 4, 1858, *Susan Brimmer Inches.*
d. Apr. 2, 1876.

ROBERT (A 12, B 1)
b. June 27, 1859.
m. June 14, 1888, *Marion Sharpless.*
d. May 3, 1900.

CHARLES INCHES (A 12, B 2)
b. July 21, 1860.
m. June 6, 1893, *Margaret Noble.*

ROGER FAXTON (A 12, B 3)
b. Mar. 21, 1862.
m. Oct. 7, 1893, *Mildred Frazer.*

HENRIETTA AUCHMUTY (A 12, B 4)
b. Mar. 11, 1864.
m. Dec. 23, 1886, *Charles Edward Ingersoll.*

ELIZABETH PERKINS (A 12, B 5)
b. Dec. 18, 1865.
m. June 2, 1885, *James Potter.*

SUSAN BRIMMER (A 12, B 6)
b. Aug. 29, 1869.
m. June 27, 1898, *Antonio Ysnaga Stewart.*

MARY HOWARD (A 12, B 7)
b. Mar. 25, 1872.
m. Feb. 28, 1898, *Edgar Thomson Scott.*

NATH'ᴸ RUSSELL STURGIS:
HIS GRANDCHILDREN AND GREAT-GRANDCHILDREN.

RUSSELL STURGIS, JR. (A 1, B 1)
b. Aug. 3, 1831.
m. July 14, 1856, *Susan Welles*
           d. Dec. 12, 1862.

m. May 29, 1866, *Margery McCulloh*.
d. Oct. 14, 1899.

RUSSELL, III. (A 1, B 1, C 1)
b. Dec. 16, 1856.
m. Mar. 30, 1880, *Anne Outram Bangs*.
d. July 17, 1899.

SUSAN WELLES (A 1, B 1, C 2)
b. July 11, 1858.
m. Oct. 26, 1886, *John Preston*.
d. Feb. 18, 1888.

RICHARD CLIPSTON (A 1, B 1, C 3)
b. Dec. 24, 1860.
m. June 22, 1882, *Esther Mary Ogden*.

WILLIAM CODMAN (A 1, B 1, C 4)
b. Nov. 15, 1862.
m. Apr. 4, 1889, *Carolyn Hall*.

SULLIVAN WARREN (A 1, B 1, C 5)
b. Apr. 24, 1868.
m. July 26, 1899, *Edith Barnes*.

EDWARD (A 1, B 1, C 6)
b. Apr. 24, 1868.

JAMES McCULLOH (A 1, B 1, C 7)
b. Nov. 13, 1872.

LUCY CODMAN (A 1, B 1, C 8)
b. Feb. 11, 1876.

8

MARY GREENE STURGIS (A 1, B 2, C 1)
b. Jan. 30, 1857.
d. Nov. 28, 1877.

CHARLES RUSSELL, JR. (A 1, B 2, C 2)
b. July 17, 1858.
d. Oct. 11, 1877.

LUCY STURGIS (A 1, B 2, C 3)
b. Apr. 3, 1860.
d. Feb. 4, 1866.

RUSSELL STURGIS (A 1, B 2, C 4)
b. Oct. 20, 1861.
m. Aug. 4, 1891, *Anna Kneeland Crafts.*

ANNE MACMASTER (A 1, B 2, C 5)
b. Nov. 11, 1864.
m. Nov. 15, 1892, *Henry Bromfield Cabot.*

SUSAN WELLES (A 1, B 2, C 6)
b. Dec. 30, 1866.
m. May 19, 1896, *Redington Fiske.*

JOHN STURGIS (A 1, B 2, C 7)
b. Feb. 25, 1868.

JULIAN (A 1, B 2, C 8)
b. Sept. 21, 1870.
m. Apr. 29, 1897, *Norah Chadwick.*

PAUL (A 1, B 2, C 9)
b. Nov. 24, 1873.
d. Aug. 6, 1875.

NATH'ᴸ RUSSELL STURGIS:
HIS GRANDCHILDREN AND
GREAT-GRANDCHILDREN.

JOHN HUBBARD STURGIS (A 1, B 3)
b. Aug. 5, 1834.
m. Sept. 14, 1858, *Frances Anne Codman.*
d. Feb. 14, 1888.

JULIAN OVERING (A 1, B 3, C 1)
b. Aug. 6, 1859.
d. Jan. 24, 1861.

JOHN HUBBARD, JR. (A 1, B 3, C 2)
b. Oct. 11, 1860.
m. July 19, 1898, *Kate Hosmer.*

GERTRUDE GOUVERNEUR (A 1, B 3, C 3)
b. Feb. 3, 1862.
m. Aug. 29, 1889, *Francis Welles Hunnewell.*
d. Mar. 15, 1890.

FRANCES CODMAN (A 1, B 3, C 4)
b. Nov. 7, 1863.

MABEL RUSSELL (A 1, B 3, C 5)
b. July 17, 1865.

ALICE MAUD RUSSELL (A 1, B 3, C 6)
b. June 4, 1868.

CHARLES RUSSELL (A 1, B 3, C 7)
b. Apr. 9, 1871.

EVELYN RUSSELL (A 1, B 3, C 8)
b. Oct. 4, 1872.

MARY GREENE STURGIS (A 1, B 4)
b. June 18, 1837.
d. Apr. 28, 1838.

ATH'ᴸ RUSSELL STURGIS: IS GRANDCHILDREN AND REAT-GRANDCHILDREN.

MARGERY (A 5, B 5, C 1)
b. June 25, 1874.
m. Jan. 31, 1900, *W. Ellice.*

RACHEL (A 5, B 5, C 2)
b. Feb. 6, 1876.
m. Sept. 8, 1898, *Aubry Price.*

OLIVE (A 5, B 5, C 3)
b. Apr. 24, 1878.

ENRY PARKMAN STURGIS (A 5, B 5)
Mar. 5, 1847.
. Oct. 2, 1872, *Mary Cecilia Brand*
            d. June 18, 1886.

HENRY RUSSELL (A 5, B 5, C 4)
b. Oct. 25, 1879.

JOHN BRYAN (A 5, B 5, C 5)
b. June 22, 1885.

MARY (A 5, B 5, C 6)
b. June 17, 1886.

JOAN MEREDITH (A 5, B 5, C 7)
b. July 24, 1895.

2. July 17, 1894, *Marie Eveleen Meredith.*

DOROTHY MEREDITH (A 5, B 5, C 8)
b. Jan. 26, 1897.

NATH'L RUSSELL STURGIS: HIS GRANDCHILDREN AND GREAT-GRANDCHILDREN.

JULIAN RUSSELL STURGIS (A 1, B 6)
b. Oct. 21, 1848.
m. Nov. 8, 1883, *Mary Maud Beresford.*

MARK BERESFORD RUSSELL (A 1, B 6, C 1)
b. July 10, 1884.

GERARD BOIT (A 1, B 6, C 2)
b. Sept. 12, 1885.

ROLAND JOSSELYN RUSSELL (A 1, B 6, C 3)
b. Jan. 9, 1888.

NATH'ᴸ RUSSELL STURGIS: HIS GRANDCHILDREN AND GREAT-GRANDCHILDREN.

MILDRED (A 1, B 7, C 1)
b. Aug. 14, 1872.

CONWAY RUSSELL (A 1, B 7, C 2)
b. June 24, 1874.
m. May 27, 1897, *Louisa Mary Street.*

RICHARD STURGIS (A 1, B 7, C 3)
b. Sept. 21, 1875.

MARY GREENE HUBBARD STURGIS (A 1, B 7)
b. Feb. 2, 1851.
m. July 5, 1871, *Leopold Richard Seymour.*

EDWARD (A 1, B 7, C 4)
b. Feb. 10, 1877.

BEAUCHAMP (A 1, B 7, C 5)
b. Oct. 6, 1878.

ETHEL (A 1, B 7, C 6)
b. Jan. 17, 1881.

LIONEL (A 1, B 7, C 7)
b. Feb. 24, 1889.

HOWARD OVERING STURGIS (A 1, B 8)
b. Nov. 8, 1855.

GEORGE ROBERT RUSSELL STURGIS (A 2, B 1)
b. May 25, 1836.
d. Dec. 11, 1865.

MARY HOWARD STURGIS (A 2, B 2)
b. Dec. 8, 1837.
d. Dec. 12, 1837.

HENRY HOWARD STURGIS (A 2, B 3)
b. Nov. 5, 1838.
m. Nov. 5, 1863, *Caroline Augusta Manson*
d. Jan. 31, 1881.   *d. Oct. 31, 1880.*

JAMES PERKINS STURGIS (A 2, B 4)
b. Oct. 29, 1839.
d. Sept. 8, 1840.

JAMES PERKINS STURGIS (A 2, B 5)
b. Oct. 14, 1841.
d. Jan. 2, 1864.

CHARLES EDWARD STURGIS (A 2, B 6)
b. July 31, 1843.
d. Aug. 4, 1843.

FREDERICK RUSSELL STURGIS (A 2, B 7)
b. July 7, 1844.
m. Apr. 6, 1870, *Martha DeWolf Hazard.*

MARY TRINIDAD HOWARD STURGIS (A 2, B 8)
b. July 26, 1848.
m. Apr. 18, 1881, *Samuel George Chetwynd Middlemore*
d. Feb. 11, 1890.   *d. Jan. 27, 1890.*

NATH'ᴸ RUSSELL STURGIS: HIS GRANDCHILDREN AND GREAT-GRANDCHILDREN.

HENRY STURGIS GREW (A 4, B 1)
b. Jan. 23, 1834.
m. Dec. 20, 1863, *Jane Norton Wigglesworth.*

HENRY STURGIS, JR. (A 4, B 1, C 1)
b. July 22, 1865.
d. Aug. 20, 1866.

EDWARD WIGGLESWORTH (A 4, B 1, C 2)
b. June 26, 1867.

JANE NORTON (A 4, B 1, C 3)
b. Sept. 20, 1868.
m. Dec. 11, 1890, *John Pierpont Morgan, Jr.*

ELIZABETH STURGIS (A 4, B 1, C 4)
b. Aug. 29, 1871.
m. Oct. 4, 1893, *Boylston Adams Beal.*

HENRIETTA MARIAN (A 4, B 1, C 5)
b. Dec. 20, 1872.
m. Sept. 18, 1895, *Stephen Van Rensselaer Crosby.*

CHARLES JAMES GREW (A 4, B 2)
b. Jan. 14, 1836.
d. Mar. 17, 1850.

NATH'ᴸ RUSSELL STURGIS:
HIS GRANDCHILDREN AND
GREAT-GRANDCHILDREN.

ROBERT STURGIS (A 4, B 3, C 1)
b. Sept. 1, 1871.
d. Aug. 10, 1872.

RANDOLPH CLARK (A 4, B 3, C 2)
b. Sept. 21, 1873.

EDWARD STURGIS GREW (A 4, B 3)
b. Mar. 10, 1842.
m. Nov. 26, 1867, *Annie Crawford Clark.*

HENRY STURGIS, II. (A 4, B 3, C 3)
b. Nov. 1, 1875,
m. Nov. 17, 1897, *Ethel Gertrude Hooper.*

JOSEPH CLARK (A 4, B 3, C 4)
b. May 27, 1880.

ELEANOR JACKSON (A 4, B 3, C 5)
b. Sept. 14, 1882.

ELIZABETH PERKINS GREW (A 4, B 4)
b. July 14, 1845.
d. Jan. 16, 1889.

NATH'ᴸ RUSSELL STURGIS:
HIS GRANDCHILDREN AND
GREAT-GRANDCHILDREN.

ODORE PARKMAN (A 5, B 5)
n. 22, 1837.
l in battle Dec. 16, 1862.

RY RUSSELL PARKMAN (A 5, B 2)
1g. 8, 1838.

AN PARKMAN (A 5, B 3)
ɔv. 6, 1839.
1e 3, 1850.

E PARKMAN (A 5, B 4)
1y 6, 1844.
n. 7, 1878, *William Smith Carter.*

{ THEODORE PARKMAN (A 5, B 4, C 5)
b. Apr. 4, 1880.

THA STURGIS PARKMAN (A 5, B 5)
ɔt. 30, 1849.
t. 14, 1875.

NATH'ᴸ RUSSELL STURGIS: HIS GRANDCHILDREN ANᴅ GREAT-GRANDCHILDREN

ANNA SHAW (A 8, B 1)
b. Apr. 9, 1836.
m. Nov. 28, 1856, *George William Curtis*
           d. Aug. 31, 1892.

FRANCIS GEORGE (A 8, B 1, C 1)
b. Dec. 5, 1857.
m. Feb. 21, 1887, *Ruth Weatherbee Davison.*

ELIZABETH BURRELL (A 8, B 1, C 2)
b. Apr. 15, 1861.

SARAH SHAW (A 8, B 1, C 3)
b. May 17, 1863.
d. Apr. 11, 1874.

ROBERT GOULD SHAW (A 8, B 2)
b. Oct. 10, 1837.
m. May 2, 1863, *Annie Haggerty.*
killed in battle July 18, 1863.

turn
889.

ROBERT SHAW (A 8, B 3, C 1)
b. Aug 21, 1863.

SARAH MAY (A 8, B 3, C 2)
b. Sept. 3, 1865.
m. Nov. 7, 1895, *Henry Dwight Sedgwick, Jr.*

EDITH (A 8, B 3, C 3)
b. June 20, 1867.
m. Aug. 20, 1895, *Isaac Newton Phelps Stokes.*

FRANCIS (A 8, B 3, C 4)
b. June 1, 1871.
d. Jan. 6, 1878.

GERTRUDE (A 8, B 3, C 5)
b. June 25, 1872.

MILDRED (A 8, B 3, C 6)
b. Nov. 19, 1875.

HUGH (A 8, B 3, C 7)
b. Sept. 20, 1882.

NATH'L RUSSELL STU
HIS GRANDCHILDREN
GREAT-GRANDCHILD

JOSEPHINE SHAW (A 8, B 4)
b. Dec. 16, 1843.
m. Oct. 30, 1863, *Charles Russell Lowell, Jr.*
    killed in battle Oct. 20, 1864.

CARLOTTA RUSSELL (A 8, B 4, C 1)
b. Nov. 30, 1864.

ROBERT SHAW (A 8, B 5, C 1)
b. July 4, 1869.

ELLEN SHAW (A 8, B 5)
b. July 1, 1845.
m. Oct. 24, 1867, *Francis Channing Barlow*
    d. Jan. 11, 1896.

CHARLES LOWELL (A 8, B 5, C 2)
b. Oct. 10, 1871.

LOUISA SHAW (A 8, B 5, C 3)
b. July 27, 1873.
m. Nov. 23, 1897, *Pierre Jay.*

2)

3)

GEORGE (A 9, B 4, C 1)
b. May 31, 1891.

WINTHROP (A 9, B 4, C 2)
b. Sept. 15, 1892.
d. Aug. 3, 1893.

MARY DONNISON (A 9, B 4, C 3)
b. Feb. 25, 1894.

JOSEPHINE (A 9, B 4, C 4)
b. May 11, 1896.

NATH'ᴸ RUSSELL STURGIS: HIS GRANDCHILDREN AND GREAT-GRANDCHILDREN.

WILLIAM HOWARD WHITE (A 10, B 1)
b. Feb. 21, 1847.
m. Oct. 8, 1878, *Margaret Parker.*
d. Dec. 11, 1895.

JOSEPH LOWELL (A 10, B 1, C 1)
b. May 14, 1880.

THEODORE PARKMAN (A 10, B 1, C 2)
b. Aug. 12, 1882.

SARAH HARRIETT (A 10, B 1, C 3)
b. Apr. 14, 1887.

AMY WHITE (A 10, B 2)
b. Sept. 25, 1848.

NATH'ᴸ RUSSELL STURGIS: HIS GRANDCHILDREN AND GREAT-GRANDCHILDREN.

USAN STURGIS (A ₅₅, B ₅)
. Sept. 7, 1846.
₁. Jan. 16, 1867, *Henry Horton McBurney*
                d. Feb. 10, 1875.

₁. May 3, 1876, *Henry Bigelow Williams.*

HARLES WILKINS STURGIS (A ₅₅, B 2)
. May 29, 1849.

RANCIS SHAW STURGIS (A ₅₅, B 3)
. Aug. 15, 1853.

MARY (A ₅₅, B ₅, C ₅)
b. Oct. 26, 1867.
m. Nov. 6, 1889, *Frederic Parker.*

THOMAS CURTIS (A ₅₅, B ₅, C 2)
b. Oct. 7, 1870.
d. Sept. 29, 1874.

MARGARET (A ₅₅, B ₅, C 3)
b. Sept. 6, 1873.
m. June 1, 1892, *Henry Remsen Whitehouse.*

NATH'L RUSSELL STURGIS
HIS GRANDCHILDREN AN
GREAT-GRANDCHILDREN

ROBERT STURGIS (A 12, B 1)
b. June 27, 1859.
m. June 14, 1888, *Marion Sharpless.*
d. May 3, 1900.

MARY LYMAN (A 12, B 1, C 1)
b. Feb. 14, 1890.

HENRIETTA HOWARD BOIT (A 12, B 1, C 2)
b. Oct. 29, 1896.

CHARLES INCHES STURGIS (A 12, B 2)
b. July 21, 1860.
m. June 6, 1893, *Margaret Noble.*

ROBERT SHAW, II. (A 12, B 2, C 1)
b. Apr. 4, 1894.

FRANK NOBLE (A 12, B 2, C 2)
b. Jan. 9, 1897.

SUSAN BRIMMER (A 12, B 3, C 1)
b. Nov. 11, 1894.

ROGER FAXTON STURGIS (A 12, B 3)
b. Mar. 21, 1862.
m. Oct. 7, 1893. *Mildred Frazer.*

ROGER (A 12, B 3, C 2)
b. Feb. 10, 1896.

ANITA (A 12, B 3, C 3)
b. June 15, 1898.

HENRIETTA AUCHMUTY STURGIS (A 12, B 4)
b. Mar. 11, 1864.
m. Dec. 23, 1886, *Charles Edward Ingersoll.*

ANNA WARREN (A 12, B 4, C 1)
b. Sept. 30, 1887.

HARRY (A 12, B 4, C 2)
b. May 27, 1890.

ROBERT STURGIS (A 12, B 4, C 3)
b. Dec. 16, 1891.

CHARLES JARED (A 12, B 4, C 4)
b. Feb. 11, 1894.

SUSAN BRIMMER (A 12, B 4, C 5)
b. Feb. 19, 1896.

JOHN HOBART WARREN (A 12, B 4, C 6)
b. Oct. 27, 1899.

ELIZABETH PERKINS STURGIS (A 12, B 5)
b. Dec. 18, 1865.
m. June 2, 1885, *James Potter*.

ELIZABETH STURGIS (A 12, B 5, C 1)
b. July 9, 1886.

JOHN HAMILTON (A 12, B 5, C 2)
b. June 13, 1888.

ROBERT STURGIS (A 12, B 5, C 3)
b. Dec. 20, 1889.

ALICE BEIRNE (A 12, B 5, C 4)
b. July 14, 1892.
d. Apr. 12, 1893.

NATH'ᴸ RUSSELL STURGIS:
HIS GRANDCHILDREN AND
GREAT-GRANDCHILDREN.

SUSAN BRIMMER STURGIS (A 12, B 6)
b. Aug. 29, 1869.
m. June 27, 1898, *Antonio Ysnaga Stewart*.

{ SUSAN BRIMMER (A 12, B 6, C 1)
b. Mar. 2, 1900.

MARY HOWARD STURGIS (A 12, B 7)
b. Mar. 25, 1872.
m. Feb. 28, 1898, *Edgar Thomson Scott*.

{ EDGAR THOMSON (A 12, B 7, C 1)
b. Jan. 11, 1899.

NATH'ᴸ RUSSELL STURGIS:
HIS GREAT-GRANDCHILDREN AND GREAT-GREAT-GRANDCHILDREN.

RUSSELL STURGIS, III. (A 1, B 1, C 1)
b. Dec. 16, 1856.
m. Mar. 30, 1880, *Anne Outram Bangs.*
d. July 17, 1899.

RUSSELL, IV. (A 1, B 1, C 1, D 1)
b. Dec. 31, 1880.

ANNE OUTRAM (A 1, B 1, C 1, D 2)
b. Mar. 25, 1882.

SUSAN WELLES (A 1, B 1, C 1, D 3)
b. Jan. 4, 1885.

BEATRICE OUTRAM (A 1, B 1, C 1, D 4)
b. Aug. 7, 1886.

GERTRUDE (A 1, B 1, C 1, D 5)
b. June 20, 1889.

CAROLYN (A 1, B 1, C 1, D 6)
b. June 16, 1891.

FRANCES (A 1, B 1, C 1, D 7)
b. Nov. 27, 1893.

NATH'L RUSSELL STURGIS:
HIS GREAT-GRANDCHILDREN AND GREAT-GREAT-GRANDCHILDREN.

SUSAN WELLES STURGIS (A 1, B 1, C 2)
b. July 11, 1858.
m. Oct. 26, 1886, *John Preston.*
d. Feb. 18, 1888.

RICHARD CLIPSTON STURGIS (A 1, B 1, C 3)
b. Dec. 24, 1860.
m. June 22, 1882, *Esther Mary Ogden.*

RICHARD CLIPSTON, JR. (A 1, B 1, C 3, D 1)
b. Mar. 17, 1884.

GEORGE OGDEN (A 1, B 1, C 3, D 2)
b. Aug. 10, 1889.
d. Aug.   , 1889.

DOROTHY MARGARET (A 1, B 1, C 3, D 3)
b. July 28, 1891.

WILLIAM CODMAN STURGIS (A 1, B 1, C 4)
b. Nov. 15, 1862.
m. Apr. 4, 1889, *Carolyn Hall.*

NORMAN ROMNEY (A 1, B 1, C 4, D 1)
b. Feb. 3, 1890.

ALAN HALL (A 1, B 1, C 4, D 2)
b. Apr. 29, 1892.

MARGARET (A 1, B 1, C 4, D 3)
b. Mar. 1, 1894.

JULIA (A 1, B 1, C 4, D 4)
b. May 23, 1898.

C 5)

η)

MARY GREENE STURGIS CODMAN (A 1, B 2, C 1)
b. Jan. 30, 1857.
d. Nov. 28, 1877.

CHARLES RUSSELL CODMAN, JR. (A 1, B 2, C 2)
b. July 17, 1858.
d. Oct. 11, 1877.

LUCY STURGIS CODMAN (A 1, B 2, C 3)
b. Apr. 3, 1860.
d. Feb. 4, 1866.

RUSSELL STURGIS CODMAN (A 1, B 2, C 4)
b. Oct. 20, 1861.
m. Aug. 4, 1891, *Anna Kneeland Crafts.*

CHARLES RUSSELL, JR. (A 1, B 2, C 4, D 1)
b. Feb. 22, 1893.

RUSSELL STURGIS, JR. (A 1, B 2, C 4, D 2)
b. June 15, 1896.

ASTER CODMAN (A 1, B 2, C 5)

Henry Bromfield Cabot.

HENRY BROMFIELD, JR. (A 1, B 2, C 5, D 1)
b. Dec. 7, 1894.

POWELL MASON (A 1, B 2, C 5, D 2)
b. Dec. 20, 1896.

PAUL CODMAN (A 1, B 2, C 5, D 3)
b. Oct. 21, 1898.

ES CODMAN (A 1, B 2, C 6)

Redington Fiske.

REDINGTON, JR. (A 1, B 2, C 6, D 1)
b. Dec. 3, 1898.

33

JOHN STURGIS CODMAN (A 1, B 2, C 7)
b. Feb. 25, 1868.

JULIAN CODMAN (A 1, B 2, C 8)
b. Sept. 21, 1870.
m. Apr. 29, 1897, Norah Chadwick.

PAUL CODMAN (A 1, B 2, C 9)
b. Nov. 24, 1873.
d. Aug. 6, 1875.

(A 1, B 3, C 1)

A 1, B 3, C 2) { GERTRUDE GOUVERNEUR (A 1, B 3, C 2, D 1)
                  b. July 5, 1899.

STURGIS (A 1, B 3, C 3)

lunne'well.

NATH'ᴸ RUSSELL STURGIS:
HIS GREAT-GRANDCHILDREN AND GREAT-GREAT-GRANDCHILDREN.

FRANCES CODMAN STURGIS (A 1, B 3, C 4)
b. Nov. 7, 1863.

MABEL RUSSELL STURGIS (A 1, B 3, C 5)
b. July 17, 1865.

ALICE MAUD RUSSELL STURGIS (A 1, B 3, C 6)
b. June 4, 1868.

CHARLES RUSSELL STURGIS (A 1, B 3, C 7)
b. Apr. 9, 1871.

EVELYN RUSSELL STURGIS (A 1, B 3, C 8)
b. Oct. 4, 1872.

B 5, C 1)

, C 2)

3)

NATH'L RUSSELL STURGIS:
HIS GREAT-GRANDCHILDREN AND
GREAT-GREAT-GRANDCHILDREN.

HENRY RUSSELL STURGIS (A 1, B 5, C 4)
b. Oct. 25, 1879.

JOHN BRYAN STURGIS (A 1, B 5, C 5)
b. June 22, 1881.

MARY STURGIS (A 1, B 5, C 6)
b. June 17, 1886.

REDITH STURGIS (A 1, B 5, C 7)
395.

MEREDITH STURGIS (A 1, B 5, C 8)
397.

NATH'ᴸ RUSSELL STURGIS: HIS GREAT-GRANDCHILDREN AND GREAT-GREAT-GRANDCHILDREN.

MARK BERESFORD RUSSELL STURGIS (A 5, B 6, C 5)
b. July 10, 1884.

GERARD BOIT STURGIS (A 5, B 6, C 2)
b. Sept. 12, 1885.

ROLAND JOSSELYN RUSSELL STURGIS (A 5, B 6, C 3)
b. Jan. 9, 1888.

CONWAY RUSSELL SEYMOUR (A 1, B 7, C 2)
b. June 24, 1874.
m. May 27, 1897, *Louisa Mary Street*.

RICHARD STURGIS SEYMOUR (A 1, B 7, C 3)
b. Sept. 21, 1875.

NATH'ᴸ RUSSELL STURGIS:
HIS GREAT-GRANDCHILDREN AND
GREAT-GREAT-GRANDCHILDREN.

EDWARD SEYMOUR (A 1, B 7, C 4)
b. Feb. 10, 1877.

BEAUCHAMP SEYMOUR (A 1, B 7, C 5)
b. Oct. 6, 1878.

ETHEL SEYMOUR (A 1, B 7, C 6)
b. Jan. 17, 1881.

LIONEL SEYMOUR (A 1, B 7, C 7)
b. Feb. 24, 1889.

HIS GREAT-GRANDCHILDREN AND
GREAT-GREAT-GRANDCHILDREN

NATH'L RUSSELL STURGIS:
HIS GREAT-GRANDCHILDREN AND GREAT-GREAT-GRANDCHILDREN.

HENRY STURGIS GREW, JR. (A 4, B 1, C 1)
b. July 22, 1865.
d. Aug. 20, 1866.

EDWARD WIGGLESWORTH GREW (A 4, B 1, C 2)
b. June 26, 1867.

JUNIUS SPENCER (A 4, B 1, C 3, D 1)
b. Mar. 15, 1892.

JANE NORTON GREW (A 4, B 1, C 3)
P. Sept. 20, 1868.
m. Dec. 11, 1890, *John Pierpont Morgan, Jr.*

JANE NORTON (A 4, B 1, C 3, D 2)
b. Nov. 14, 1893.

FRANCES TRACY (A 4, B 1, C 3, D 3)
b. Jan. 17, 1897.

ELIZABETH STURGIS GREW (A 4, B 1, C 4)
b. Aug. 29, 1871.
m. Oct. 4, 1893, *Boylston Adams Beal.*

{ ELIZABETH STURGIS (A 4, B 1, C 4, D 1)
b. July 4, 1899.

HENRIETTA MARIAN GREW (A 4, B 1, C 5)
b. Dec. 20, 1872.
m. Sept. 18, 1895, *Stephen Van Rensselaer Crosby.*

{ HENRY GREW (A 4, B 1, C 5, D 1)
b. June 4, 1898.

NATH'L RUSSELL STURGIS: HIS GREAT-GRANDCHILDREN AND GREAT-GREAT-GRANDCHILDREN.

ROBERT STURGIS GREW (A 4, B 3, C 1)
b. Sept. 1, 1871.
d. Aug. 10, 1872.

RANDOLPH CLARK GREW (A 4, B 3, C 2)
b. Sept. 21, 1873.

HENRY STURGIS GREW, II. (A 4, B 3, C 3)   { AGNES HOPPIN (A 4, B 3, C 3, D 1)
b. Nov. 1, 1875.   { b. Nov. 13, 1898.
m. Nov. 17, 1897, *Ethel Gertrude Hooper.*

JOSEPH CLARK GREW (A 4, B 3, C 4)
b. May 27, 1880.

ELEANOR JACKSON GREW (A 4, B 3, C 5)
b. Sept. 14, 1882.

ODORE PARKMAN CARTER (A 5, B 4, C 1)
r. 4, 1880.

NATH'ᴸ RUSSELL STURGIS: HIS GREAT-GRANDCHILDREN AND GREAT-GREAT-GRANDCHILDREN.

FRANCIS GEORGE CURTIS (A 8, B 1, C 1)
b. Dec. 5, 1857.
m. Feb. 21, 1887, *Ruth Weatherbee Davison.*

FRANCIS SHAW (A 8, B 1, C 1, D 1)
b. June 10, 1889.

MARGARET BURRILL (A 8, B 1, C 1, D 2)
b. Apr. 27, 1890.

EDWARD DAVISON (A 8, B 1, C 1, D 3)
b. Dec. 20, 1891.

GEORGE WILLIAM (A 8, B 1, C 1, D 4)
b. Mar. 29, 1895.

ELIZABETH BURRELL CURTIS (A 8, B 1, C 2)
b. Apr. 15, 1861.

SARAH SHAW CURTIS (A 8, B 1, C 3)
b. May 17, 1863.
d. Apr. 11, 1874.

MINTURN (A 8, B 3, C 2)

Henry Dwight Sedgwick, Jr.

HENRY DWIGHT, III. (A 8, B 3, C 2, D 1)
b. Sept. 6, 1896.

ROBERT MINTURN (A 8, B 3, C 2, D 2)
b. Jan. 27, 1899.

JRN (A 8, B 3, C 3)

. Isaac Newton Phelps Stokes.

NATH'L RUSSELL STURGIS: HIS GREAT-GRANDCHILDREN AND GREAT-GREAT-GRANDCHILDREN.

FRANCIS MINTURN (A 8, B 3, C 4)
b. June 1, 1871.
d. Jan. 6, 1878.

GERTRUDE MINTURN (A 8, B 3, C 5)
b. June 25, 1872.

MILDRED MINTURN (A 8, B 3, C 6)
b. Nov. 19, 1875.

HUGH MINTURN (A 8, B 3, C 7)
b. Sept. 20, 1882.

LOWELL (A 8, B 4, C 1)

NATH'ᴸ RUSSELL STURGIS:
HIS GREAT-GRANDCHILDREN AND
GREAT-GREAT-GRANDCHILDREN.

ROBERT SHAW BARLOW (A 8, B 5, C 1)
b. July 4, 1869.

CHARLES LOWELL BARLOW (A 8, B 5, C 2)
b. Oct. 10, 1871.

LOUISA SHAW BARLOW (A 8, B 5, C 3)
b. July 27, 1873.
m. Nov. 23, 1897, *Pierre Jay.*

{ **ELLEN** (A 8, B 5, C 3, D 1)
b. Aug. 23, 1899.

GIS (A 9, B 4, C 1)

URGIS (A 9, B 4, C 2)

SÒN STURGIS (A 9, B 4, C 3)

JRGIS (A 9, B 4, C 4)

JOSEPH LOWELL WHITE (A 10, B 1, C 1)
b. May 14, 1880.

THEODORE PARKMAN WHITE (A 10, B 1, C 2)
b. Aug. 12, 1882.

SARAH HARRIETT WHITE (A 10, B 1, C 3)
b. Apr. 14, 1887.

ELIZABETH (A 11, B 1, C 1, D 2)
b. Nov. 17, 1891.

MARY McBURNEY (A 11, B 1, C 1)
b. Oct. 26, 1867.
m. Nov. 6, 1889, *Frederic Parker.*

HENRY McBURNEY (A 11, B 1, C 1, D 3)
b. Apr. 11, 1893.

THOMAS (A 11, B 1, C 1, D 4)
b. Apr. 20, 1898.
d. Aug. 30, 1898.

MARY (A 11, B 1, C 1, D 5)
b. Oct. 4, 1899.

THOMAS CURTIS McBURNEY (A 11, B 1, C 2)
b. Oct. 7, 1870.
d. Sept. 29, 1874.

MARGARET McBURNEY (A 11, B 1, C 3)
b. Sept. 6, 1873.
m. June 1, 1892, *Henry Remsen Whitehouse.*

BEATRIX (A 11, B 1, C 3, D 1)
b. July 9, 1893.

MARY LYMAN STURGIS (A 12, B 1, C 1)
b. Feb. 14, 1890.

HENRIETTA HOWARD BOIT STURGIS (A 12, B 1, C 2)
b. Oct. 29, 1896.

ROBERT SHAW STURGIS, II. (A 12, B 2, C 1)
b. Apr. 4, 1894.

FRANK NOBLE STURGIS (A 12, B 2, C 2)
b. Jan. 9, 1897.

NATH'ᴸ RUSSELL STURGIS:
HIS GREAT-GRANDCHILDREN.

SUSAN BRIMMER STURGIS (A 12, B 3, C 1)
b. Nov. 11, 1894.

ROGER STURGIS (A 12, B 3, C 2)
b. Feb. 10, 1896.

ANITA STURGIS (A 12, B 3, C 3)
b. June 15, 1898.

ANNA WARREN INGERSOLL (A 12, B 4, C 1)
b. Sept. 30, 1887.

HARRY INGERSOLL (A 12, B 4, C 2)
b. May 27, 1890.

ROBERT STURGIS INGERSOLL (A 12, B 4, C 3)
b. Dec. 16, 1891.

NATH'ᴸ RUSSELL STURGIS:
HIS GREAT-GRANDCHILDREN.

CHARLES JARED INGERSOLL (A 12, B 4, C 4)
b. Feb. 11, 1894.

SUSAN BRIMMER INGERSOLL (A 12, B 4, C 5)
b. Feb. 19, 1896.

JOHN HOBART WARREN INGERSOLL (A 12, B 4, C 6)
b. Oct. 27, 1899.

͏BETH STURGIS POTTER (A 12, B 5, C 1)
͏9, 1886.

͏ HAMILTON POTTER (A 12, B 5, C 2)
͏ 13, 1888.

͏RT STURGIS POTTER (A 12, B 5, C 3)
͏. 20, 1889.

͏ BEIRNE POTTER (A 12, B 5, C 4)
͏ 14, 1892.
͏. 12, 1893.

SUSAN BRIMMER STEWART (A 12, B 6, C 1)
b. Mar. 2, 1900.